CW00432409

1

Bored Planet

S. J. Leman

A selection of poems written by an autistic mind. Different ways of thinking and an insight to a bored mind with a life from a different planet.

Raising awareness and acceptance of autism with #boredplanet through questions, art and alternative ways.

Start the discussion and question my words.

To Colby, forever missed

Contents

11

The Purpose of Man

The purpose of man
Is to give man a purpose

Words wisen us to the thoughts
of others

Songs steal questions
We'll still never understand

For

Not to search is not to find
To search is to hope to find
To find is to hope to understand

No search is no purpose
And the opposite is true

When does a Stripe Become a Stripe?

When does a stripe become a
stripe?
A dot a hole the seen to sight
A dash a line a margin fine
Stripes are straight but also what
Wavy curved can't tell me not
Write on lines or unseen space
Is a stripe the space between
Or does create the stripe the
space
Size could count or maybe not
Objective description yes but
what

The words they use will soon
mean more
Ambiguity lacks certainty for
sure
Or is it mere subjective
definition
An eye define to hold a line
The meaning meant by that who
made
That not by logic makes no
sense
My stripe could be your
wooden fence
Objective seen objectively
Yet subjective defines reality
Yearn for sparks of creativity
If it makes me me it makes you
you

16

Maybe life holds something
more
These stripes and sparks led all
to war
Beauty, art, music, they all came
before
Who knew one stripe held such
infinite awe
But stripe became stripe, the
mix beyond me
A stripe two dimensional
infinity.

Anticlockwise

Line after line after line after
line up line shared line
Line after line shared line after
line after line

Forget shared line after line
after line
Up line after line shared line
after line after line

Forget shared line after line
after line
Up line after line shared line
after line after line

Forget shared line after line
after line

Up line after line after line after
line after line shared line

A Poem's Argument

This line doesn't exist yet
This is the first line
I am the third line
Nonsense, for the third line is I!
So I is the third line?
No; I am the third line.
Now I have four third lines
Then clearly three third lines are
wrong
But that leaves the third as the
second
Well then add another line and
Accept the second is wrong.

Pick a card

Pick a card, any card, from my
magician's deck
No joker though for it's no joke;
I hope I've made it clear
I know the card you picked, any
chance it's black or red?
Keep thinking of that card you
picked though I can't read your
mind
Think and don't forget your card
or I can't prove me right.

Number, letter possibly? Upside
down heart two three, crown?
If I've got it wrong yet please I
beg, please don't read ahead

Do you know how many cards,
how many people just gave up?
Not you, dear reader, though
you could, but may not know
now why,
For number it is probably but
that is not my act.

I know your card for I know all
but how you don't know yet
How can one know all for sure
should be your question next.
Must you try to think outside
the box with card still in your
head?
I already told your card, to you
and all alike

But it's not my deck that's
magic, it's me, not deck, not
quite.

The clue is really I know all but
first confused my words
This riddle I will answer now, I
know the card you picked
I know every card I hold, I
know of all of them.
For to know every one and all
the secret I possess

Close your mind and limit life,
then you'll know all that's left.

Guess

This word one syllable, guess at
each round
By round I mean stanza, for
each new has a clue
This verse doesn't count, or
maybe it does
Think of this word and good
luck.

Together this word with so
many can't be
Positive or negative not
necessarily
Subjective and objective, maybe
just to me
Link words with mine, now do
you see?

Answer or question both it can
do
More question? More answer?
That's up to you
See what I did there? Why not
answer that?
An answer can question, can a
poem wear a hat?

Repeat, repeat, repeat each way
The end result you mould like
clay
Am I mixing the clues, too
hard? Do say
But my answer is your question
in a way.

Are you confused? Are you
fine?

I knew your answers before I
wrote that line
Guessed the word? If yes you're
wrong
Get it? Now enjoy this twist

Do you know the word?

A Poem

A poem is no more than the
reader's view
Right now that reader is you
Interpret what follows as you
must do
This introductory monologue is
yours too

Alliteration seen in lavishly
long lingering lines
Longingly laying luxurious
literacy that almost rhymes

Or rhyming and timing
Needing speeding for reading

Praying
Or not
Explaining
Mnemonic

Hidden meanings so nearly lost
have been
A sonnet so often for love ends
scene

C   N   R   T
   O   C   E   E

Minimalist, minimalism

Or simple stanza

If wanted iambic pentameter

Repetition, repetition, repetition
is good

Like a metaphor but a simile

A garnish a flourish, some
discombobulating words

("punctuation!")

Pull from this your poem like a
fading dream
Poetry is nothing if there's no
one to read
No incorrect understanding tell
teachers what you will

And let them prove you wrong.

Today Tomorrow's Yesterday

Today tomorrow's yesterday
Tomorrow unknown pasts future
today
Yesterday fading for futures
today
Dreams of hope held in present
past
Live in future hope always
comes last
Live in past and give present
hope
Live in present though present
has passed
Present past future dreams of
tomorrow

So dark past in present live with
hope
For future tomorrow never we
know
Tomorrow a dream past fading
away
Today past or future today we
stay
Stay eternal in this fading dream

Chasing forever tomorrow's
hope

Choose to Give

Choose to give, or
Be honoured to get

But never both, for

You'll get what they've given
But give all you've got

Why do we read?

Why do we read? To say we
have read
To say to have said. Said we
have read.
But what have you said? All
that you read
All that you read you read to say
to have said
To say to said to read to read
To set to show we read we know
We know we read by what we
said
We said we read to show we
know
But to have said we read we
show, don't know
To read to say to see to be

The who, what, whys to
question the said
Read, said, past, black letter
grey
Read what's read, see what's
said
But read to see, grey green say.
Read the read to read the read
Say to see, say again the said
Change the said by knowledge
read
Always read and say unsaid
For 2 follows 1 and 3 and 4
Read and say, 2, 3, 4, change.

Schrodinger's Cat

Schrodinger's cat, both dead
and alive
Both dead and alive? Either live
or dead!
Neither dead nor live more than
possibly
Each can't be other than
potentially.

Together two maybes make one
for sure
So maybes are half, yet
certainly wrong
But uncertain truth could mean
minus one
Truth always whole at one
hundred or one

Hang on, I noticed, unknown
wrong is half
True more or less but essentially
yes
Whole unknown guess average
fifty percent
So untrue and true make wrong
half and half

Possible maybes, untrue
certainties
This is insane, It's a mere
guessing game
One answer or two, time makes
them both true
The wonderful whimsical way
of ~~life~~ CATS

To the Woman in the Car

To the woman in the car our
meeting was barely brief,
I noticed your reflection coming
up beside me.
Thinking of you now, I wish
you all the best.
Hope your day is joyous, happy,
lovely.
Unless an unpredictable sadness
occurs,
Then I give you my best wishes
and the strength to carry on.
Even if you turn out cruel and
hateful

I pray be gentle, no intention
bad, but blessed become
benevolent.
Dearest woman whom I may
never know;
If kind and happy I wish you
well,
If kind or cruel but sad, I offer
you strength,
If cruel and happy I pray;
change your way.
Attend to cruelty and sadness,
the length of joy will follow.

For you may be gone from my
life, but still exist in yours.

Eve

A mind blessed with possibility
Sitting atop the tallest tree
A waterfall of flowers flowing
Each thought turning bud to
bloom
Abundances of ripened fruit
Fields of ever-golden wheat
Roses climbing, heavens scent

From the only tree she waits
Branches bent to build her seat
No fruit had ever touched her
lips
Though still it grew never could
she taste
Out of reach 'til one blessed day
A glorious, sensual, cursed day

For now fruit grows so she can
feast

She grows to eat, engorge
herself
An endless rotting decay
beneath
Roses wrapped in their own
thorns
Autumn comes as autumn
should
Leaves falling from that lonely
tree
A woman now old lays inside
Within a prison of branches she
built.

A Castle Is Built

A castle is built
I know not when
Built before birth

Unquestioned adoption
Golden frame, coloured glass
No questions, complex
innocence

Fear of fading fantasy
Clung to unclaimed brick
Lusting barbed wire walls

Impure love unwavering
Terrifying beautiful room
Grains of sand to an oyster

Simple knowledge of laid brick
Purity of innocence
Destruction to creation

Place brick of unknown nature
Brick of castle and wall alike
Future begging look behind

Broken glass, smashed colour
No marble unused to build
Gargoyles alone remain

I built wall of certain purpose
Higher protection, lower protect
My freedom with castle
destruction

Lonely walls remain alone
Manipulated brick me

Freedom walls and gargoyles

Walls my definition
Yet lack or barbed wire
Cement loosen and my own
castle build

Puzzle

Puzzle
P ice
Pu tog there
P laced own e
Pi c t urn dse

Between Each Memory

Between each memory there's a
moment I forgot
Every feeling I've had I've also
had not

Senses and viewpoints I've had
it all
Years of forced poetry, rhyming
at school

Books I love most the first ink
to fade
Love running through fingers,
impending loss made

We only know truly when we
truly are

Remembering looking back
from afar

Things only happen once they
have been
Change only happens when it
can't be seen

Time changes nothing and time
changes all
Diving into philosophy like
punching a wall

Changing and forgetting are one
and the same
Accept the moment, forget it,
make it again

Boxes

A prized
possession every
thought

Every thought a
prized
possession

Your knowledge
sculpted the
walls

The sculpted
walls your
knowledge

You need all
you know

You know all
you need

Complete depth
of each
component

Depth complete
of each
component

You do know	You don't know
what you don't	what you do
Complexity of	Relief of
relief	complexity
Unsure	Accepting
accepting reality	unsure reality
Will your mind	Your mind will
blow	blow
Does one want	One doesn't
to leave	want to leave
My door locked	Locked my door

One box a frustration, one box a
destination

The key in the wrong door
A mistake similarly destroying
opposites.

Innocence of Creativity

Innocence of creativity
Pile numbered blocks of society
We know all we need
In that we know it all

Ignorance of the external
Counting coins, paying the
mortgage
The outside lost in boredom
The forgotten of all that was
discarded

Insecurities our anger
Cruelty has no reason
In your ignorance
Externalise and see the truth

Influence our purpose
More and more we're told
More of what you'll finally ask
More innocent creativity

In old age wisdom comes
We see how it should have been
Knowledge innocence of child
Depth and wisdom time

I refuse to hate
For the ability to hate
I would not like to possess
Reasons not understood are
reasons nonetheless

Sunflowers

Sunflower beauty shine a
yellowish light
Eternal girl with an infinite
mind
Hummingbird thoughts flash so
bright
Held and forgotten watch the
cotton unwind

Thinking and feeling one and
the same
Colours shining in unknown
rain
All forgiven yet forgotten
remain

Sunshine she is, dark in
beautiful brain.

Build resistance in moments
forgiven
With each brick her time does
pass
Stair's intention, ascend to
heaven
Sunflower trapped in
transparent glass.

Existentialism echoes
Mind's recurring shadows
Time draws the bow
Single thought struck by arrow

Amber eyes fall on thinking
rock

Knowing in truth false reality
Let go, let go, untangle this knot
Tears of leaves from weeping
tree
The arrow holds this withering
flower
Brown and lifeless petals fall
Each step hurts the fading
sunflower
Feeling all of no feeling at all.

The knot inside holds her tight
Arrow and rope together
mortality
Rain upon rain in the dark of
night
Rotting sunflower weeps seeds
of infinity.

A Raindrop

A raindrop splashing on the
ground
One raindrop makes the world
go round
Raindrop soaked in sodden soil
Babbling brook, running river
Its journey's end not at the sea
Though tides will come and
tides will go
One raindrop by the moon does
flow
That interstellar celestial sight
Watching on the world at night
Phases, eclipses, coincidences
With no movement of droplet
the world is wasted
But as I said the story's not done

Droplet evaporated by the sun
The sun that keeps the world in
place
Moving droplet in never ending
space
Clouds white and silky grey
Jet streams, whirlpools,
hurricanes
Smaller than the sun may be
But so much more distracted are
we
Minute unimaginable
consequence
Single still massive
consequence
A raindrop splashing on the
ground,
One raindrop makes the world
go round

Beauty

Beauty such a difficult word to
describe
Connotate, negotiate, analyse,
prophesise

Eternal elegance, pretty,
handsome
No one definition holds full
passive passion

Wind in long hair running
through fields
Gay joyous laughter, stunning
smiles

Pearls once an itch in an oyster
shell

Beauty an angel from heaven
fell

Glory lost wing at touch of
ground
Beyond earth and air beauty is
found

Smile away sweet lady in chains
Through torment and dungeons
your beauty was made.

One Question Deeper

One question deeper, that's all
our lives need
Nature is dying, plant more
dying trees
Hysteria found in female nature
Dead men still stronger than
those who dare talk
Poor abuse systems while
treated poorly
Minorities scared of their
protection
Cutting pollution surely helping
trees
Sexism, prejudice ruining lives
Running from racism, law's
synonym
Society moulds inequality

Individual cases making such
sense
Numbers don't lie, lots of little
is lots

The Incurable Optimist

Any lesson loved
Every success held not kept

Treasure all moments

Grateful for each sunset
The hopeful knowing of sunrise

Concrete never stopped a
thought

Logically defying logic with
hope
25 rounding to 100 with only
half

Any number, circumstance 100

The incurable optimist
Curable but never cured

Why cure the hope of man?

Pot of Gold

Seed to thought, tree to
philosophy,
Nature is given but nurture we
choose.
A plot of earth given, our truth
unveiled.
To feed the flower and live in
beauty
The balanced leaves morality
Politics the direction dictating
stem
Fine and intricate the roots, the
facts we can't deny
Yet the ungrounded, undivided,
understanding
Some call it reality, some
insanity

The nurture; light and rain.
Truth in its fullest form a
rainbow
If only we could find the pot of
gold.

Elijah's Wisdom

Why will God no longer talk to
man
Because man won't listen,
Or because man has nothing to
say.

God's words only understood
through man.
Man won't listen so man can't
say,
Yet man will preach himself
God.

Injustice spoken, the most
Powerful argument
But in man's breath of life was
an element of God

Partially shared omniscience,
omnipotence.

God's mere copper scales
dictating life
Good compliments bad,
undoing God's good.
Lack of omnibenevolence
justifying our unjust.

An ox's death left a poor
innocent grief
Bargaining with the angel of
death
If the man were to die the oxen
would follow.

The ability to plead with
certainty

Proving the good we forgot.
A man's egocentric agenda not.

All visionaries fighting to climb
the ladder
Not money, enlightenment
found at the top.
It was baggage left on the path
to search

Good is a learnt idea, could God
be too?
Could one learn that all is good?
Would that be the messiah or
every uncorrupted child?

Thoughts So Deep

Thoughts so deep I forgot to see
Reality crumbling around me
One focal point a shadow hiding
The sparkles of madness
surrounding
Alive, awake? What have I
become
Eyelashes heavy with light of
sun
Thoughts so confusing yet so
empty
Mind relaxed focused intensity
Nothing and something I
become
Numbers and matrices, zeros
and ones
Into myself I sink down down

Lower, slower? down down
down
Infinite mind can be filled with
no thing
Down down, distant voices ring
Spiralling wildly a bird's broken
wing
Chaos and madness seem too
slow
This exponential horror grows
I've fallen so deep, rested in
sand
Falling infinity sifts through my
hand
A clock my only company
Tick tick torturing me
So long I've held on for it to
end

A blink and it's gone, partially
forgotten
Struggle to quicksand,
remember to forgot.

Millions

Millions seen through just a few
Half against the final view
Half don't have the choice to
vote
Believe in only half a quote
Half of half and half again
See the ties of smiling men

Those we chose chosen for us
From millions a few to numbers
plus
In other lands the rules are mad
In this mind reality sad
Without computers ads and such
Be rid the scam that rules so
much

Halve the halves until you find
Rounded up a simple mind
Half again and then you'll find
The one who leaves us all
behind

Shapes

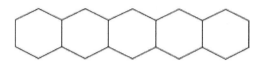

This is Not a Poem, Just Me

A stripe to star or box maybe,
Hexagonal tessellations, 360 to
3

Embellish a few;
Add a line or 2

Opinions or none
Of all things I ask 1

Question me
Online for free

Words, colours, paintings,
answers.

Abstract, feedback, comments
good and bad.
If you don't know then I may
know.
Ask or tell me why.

#boredplanet

Printed in Great Britain
by Amazon